PLANT BASED DIET

COOKBOOK

BREAKFAST RECIPES

Quick, Easy and Delicious Recipes
for a lifelong Health

Amanda Grant

Copyright © 2021 by Amanda Grant

TABLE OF CONTENTS

Breakfasts Recipes

Berry Beet Velvet Smoothie

Servings: 1

Cooking Time: 0 Minute

Ingredients:

- ➢ 1/2 of frozen banana
- ➢ 1 cup mixed red berries, 1 Medjool date, pitted
- ➢ 1 small beet, peeled, chopped
- ➢ 1 tablespoon cacao powder
- ➢ 1 teaspoon chia seeds
- ➢ 1/4 teaspoon vanilla extract, unsweetened
- ➢ 1/2 teaspoon lemon juice
- ➢ 2 teaspoons coconut butter
- ➢ 1 cup coconut milk, unsweetened

Directions:

- ➢ Place all the ingredients in the order in a food processor or blender and then pulse for 2 to 3 minutes at high speed until smooth.
- ➢ Pour the smoothie into a glass and then serve.

Nutrition Info: Calories: 234 Cal ;Fat: 5 g :Carbs: 42 g ;Protein: 11 g ;Fiber: 7 g

Spice Trade Beans And Bulgur

Servings: 10

Cooking Time: 2 Hours

Ingredients:

- ➢ 3 tablespoons canola oil, isolated
- ➢ 2 medium onions, slashed
- ➢ 1 medium sweet red pepper, slashed
- ➢ 5 garlic cloves, minced
- ➢ 1 tablespoon ground cumin
- ➢ 1 tablespoon paprika
- ➢ 2 teaspoons ground ginger
- ➢ 1 teaspoon pepper
- ➢ 1/2 teaspoon ground cinnamon
- ➢ 1/2 teaspoon cayenne pepper
- ➢ 1-1/2 cups bulgur
- ➢ 1 can (28 ounces) squashed tomatoes
- ➢ 1 can (14-1/2 ounces) diced tomatoes, undrained
- ➢ 1 container (32 ounces) vegetable juices
- ➢ 2 tablespoons darker sugar
- ➢ 2 tablespoons soy sauce
- ➢ 1 can (15 ounces) garbanzo beans or chickpeas, flushed and depleted
- ➢ 1/2 cup brilliant raisins

➢ Minced crisp cilantro, discretionary

Directions:

➢ In a large skillet, heat 2 tablespoons oil over medium-high warmth. Include onions and pepper; cook and mix until delicate, 3-4 minutes. Include garlic and seasonings; cook brief longer. Move to a 5-qt. slow cooker.

➢ In the same skillet, heat remaining oil over medium-high warmth. Include bulgur; cook and mix until daintily caramelized, 3 minutes or until softly sautéed.

➢ Include bulgur, tomatoes, stock, darker sugar, and soy sauce to slow cooker. Cook, secured, on low 4 hours or until bulgur is delicate. Mix in beans and raisins; cook 30 minutes longer. Whenever wanted, sprinkle with cilantro.

Nutrition Info: Calories: 245 Cal ;Fat: 6 g :Carbs: 45 g ;Protein: 8 g ;Fiber: 8 g

Classic Tofu Scramble

Servings: 2

Cooking Time: 15 Minutes

Ingredients:

- ➢ 1 tablespoon olive oil
- ➢ 6 ounces extra-firm tofu, pressed and crumbled
- ➢ 1 cup baby spinach
- ➢ Sea salt and ground black pepper to taste
- ➢ 1/2 teaspoon turmeric powder
- ➢ 1/4 teaspoon cumin powder
- ➢ 1/2 teaspoon garlic powder
- ➢ 1 handful fresh chives, chopped

Directions:

- ➢ Heat the olive oil in a frying skillet over medium heat. When it's hot, add the tofu and sauté for 8 minutes, stirring occasionally to promote even cooking.
- ➢ Add in the baby spinach and aromatics and continue sautéing an additional 1 to minutes.
- ➢ Garnish with fresh chives and serve warm. Bon appétit!

Nutrition Info: Per Serving: Calories: 202; Fat: 14.3g; Carbs: 7.5g; Protein: 14.6g

Almond & Raisin Granola

Servings: 8

Cooking Time: 20 Minutes

Ingredients:

- ➤ 5 ½ cups old-fashioned oats
- ➤ 1 ½ cups chopped walnuts
- ➤ ½ cup shelled sunflower seeds
- ➤ 1 cup golden raisins
- ➤ 1 cup shaved almonds
- ➤ 1 cup pure maple syrup
- ➤ ½ tsp ground cinnamon
- ➤ ¼ tsp ground allspice
- ➤ A pinch of salt

Directions:

- ➤ Preheat oven to 325 F. In a baking dish, place the oats, walnuts and sunflower seeds. Bake for minutes. Lower the heat from the oven to 300 F. Stir in the raisins, almonds, maple syrup, cinnamon, allspice, and salt. Bake for an additional 15 minutes. Allow to cool before serving.

Nutrition Info: Calories: 270 Cal ;Fat: 9 g :Carbs: 43 g ;Protein: 7 g ;Fiber: 5 g

Pumpkin And Oatmeal Bars

Servings: 3

Cooking Time: 30 Minutes

Ingredients:

- ➢ 3 cups thick oatmeal
- ➢ 1 cup seedless dates
- ➢ ½ cup of boiling water
- ➢ 2 teaspoons pumpkin pie spice
- ➢ 1 tablespoon ground flaxseed or chia seeds
- ➢ ¼ cup small sliced nuts (optional)
- ➢ ¼ cup of vegetable milk
- ➢ 1 cup mashed pumpkin

Directions:

- ➢ Preheat the oven to 350 degrees Fahrenheit.
- ➢ Cut the date into small pieces, put them in a bowl, and pour hot water. Rest for 10 minutes.
- ➢ Add dry ingredients to the bowl and mix well.
- ➢ Add dates to the dry ingredients along with water, pumpkins, and plant milk and mix well.
- ➢ Cover the square bread with baking paper and push the mixture firmly into the bread.
- ➢ Cook for 15-20 minutes.

➢ Allow the mixture to cool completely in the container, then cut into 16 squares or 8 large bars.

➢ Store in the refrigerator for up to 7 days.

Nutrition Info: Calories: 256 Cal ;Fat: 13 g :Carbs: 39 g ;Protein: 5 g ;Fiber: 4 g

Vegetarian Breakfast Casserole

Servings: 4

Cooking Time: 35 Minutes

Ingredients:

- ➢ 5 medium potatoes, about 22 ounces, boiled
- ➢ 10 ounces silken tofu
- ➢ 5 ounces tempeh, cubed
- ➢ 1 tablespoon chives, cut into rings
- ➢ 1 medium white onion, peeled chopped
- ➢ ¾ teaspoon ground black pepper
- ➢ 1 ½ teaspoon salt
- ➢ 1 teaspoon turmeric
- ➢ 2 1/2 teaspoons paprika powder
- ➢ 1 1/2 tablespoons olive oil
- ➢ 1 tablespoon corn starch
- ➢ 1 teaspoon soy sauce, 1 tablespoon barbecue sauce, 1/2 teaspoon liquid smoke
- ➢ 1/2 cup vegan cheese

Directions:

- ➢ Switch on the oven, then set it to 350 degrees F and let it preheat.
- ➢ Meanwhile, peel the boiled potatoes, then cut them into cubes and set aside until required.

➢ Prepare tempeh and for this, take a skillet pan, place it over medium heat, add half of the oil, and when hot, add half of the onion and cook for 1 minute.

➢ Then add tempeh pieces, season with 1 teaspoon paprika, add soy sauce, liquid smoke and BBQ sauce, season with salt and black pepper and cook tempeh for 5 minutes, set aside until required.

➢ Take a large skillet pan, place it over medium heat, add remaining oil and onion and cook for 2 minutes until beginning to soften.

➢ Then add potatoes, season with ½ teaspoon paprika, salt, and black pepper to taste and cook for 5 minutes until crispy, set aside until required.

➢ Take a medium bowl, place tofu in it, then add remaining ingredients and whisk until smooth.

➢ Take a casserole dish, place potatoes and tempeh in it, top with tofu mixture, sprinkle some more cheese, and bake for 20 minutes until done.

➢ Serve straight away.

Nutrition Info: Calories: 212 Cal ;Fat: 7 g :Carbs: 28 g ;Protein: 11 g ;Fiber: 5 g

Vegan Banh Mi

Servings: 4

Cooking Time: 35 Minutes

Ingredients:

- 1/2 cup rice vinegar
- 1/4 cup water
- 1/4 cup white sugar
- 2 carrots, cut into 1/16-inch-thick matchsticks
- 1/2 cup white (daikon radish, cut into 1/16-inch-thick matchsticks
- 1 white onion, thinly sliced
- 2 tablespoons olive oil
- 12 ounces firm tofu, cut into sticks
- 1/4 cup vegan mayonnaise
- 1 ½ tablespoons soy sauce
- 2 cloves garlic, minced
- 1/4 cup fresh parsley, chopped
- Kosher salt and ground black pepper, to taste
- 2 standard French baguettes, cut into four pieces
- 4 tablespoons fresh cilantro, chopped
- 4 lime wedges

Directions:

➢ Bring the rice vinegar, water and sugar to a boil and stir until the sugar has dissolved, about minute. Allow it to cool.

➢ Pour the cooled vinegar mixture over the carrot, daikon radish and onion; allow the vegetables to marinate for at least 30 minutes.

➢ While the vegetables are marinating, heat the olive oil in a frying pan over medium-high heat. Once hot, add the tofu and sauté for 8 minutes, stirring occasionally to promote even cooking.

➢ Then, mix the mayo, soy sauce, garlic, parsley, salt and ground black pepper in a small bowl.

➢ Slice each piece of the baguette in half the long way Then, toast the baguette halves under the preheated broiler for about 3 minutes.

➢ To assemble the banh mi sandwiches, spread each half of the toasted baguette with the mayonnaise mixture; fill the cavity of the bottom half of the bread with the fried tofu sticks, marinated vegetables and cilantro leaves.

➢ Lastly, squeeze the lime wedges over the filling and top with the other half of the baguette. Bon appétit!

Nutrition Info: Per Serving: Calories: 372; Fat: 21.9g; Carbs: 29.5g; Protein: 17.6g

Blueberry Smoothie Bowl

Servings: 2

Cooking Time: 5 Minutes

Ingredients:

- 1 tbsp. ground flaxseed
- 1 medium banana
- 4 ice cubes
- 1 cup blueberries
- ¾ cup unsweetened almond milk
- 1 tbsp. maple syrup
- ¼ cup nuts chopped

Directions:

- Blend all ingredients in high speed blender.
- The mixture will be rather thick so make sure you have a good high-speed blender.
- If you prefer a thinner consistency add more almond milk.
- Garnish with chopped nuts and mint leaves.
- Serve and enjoy!

Nutrition Info: Calories: 398 Cal ;Fat: 9 g :Carbs: 27 g ;Protein: 6 g ;Fiber: 4 g

Almond Oatmeal Porridge

Servings: 4

Cooking Time: 25 Minutes

Ingredients:

➢ 2 ½ cups vegetable broth

➢ 2 ½ cups almond milk

➢ ½ cup steel-cut oats

➢ 1 tbsp pearl barley

➢ ½ cup slivered almonds

➢ ¼ cup nutritional yeast

➢ 2 cups old-fashioned rolled oats

Directions:

➢ Pour the broth and almond milk in a pot over medium heat and bring to a boil. Stir in oats, pearl barley, almond slivers, and nutritional yeast. Reduce the heat and simmer for 20 minutes. Add in the rolled oats, cook for an additional 5 minutes, until creamy. Allow to cool before serving.

Nutrition Info: Calories: 250 Cal ;Fat: 6 g :Carbs: 45 g ;Protein: 6 g ;Fiber: 2 g

The Quick And Easy Bowl Of Oatmeal For Breakfast

Servings: 2

Cooking Time: 5 Minutes

Ingredients:

➢ ½ cup of quick oatmeal

➢ ½ - ⅔ cup of hot or cold water

➢ ½ cup of vegetable milk

➢ 1 teaspoon of maqui berry powder or acai powder (optional)

➢ ½ cup of fresh grapes or berries

➢ banana (or a whole banana, if you prefer)

➢ Walnuts, Seeds

Directions:

➢ Combine oatmeal and water in a bowl, and let them soak for a few minutes.

➢ Cut the banana and grapes or berries as you wish, and add them to the oatmeal.

➢ Pour vegetable milk over oatmeal and fruits.

➢ Cover with nuts, seeds, powdered maqui berry or acai powder. I use walnuts and hemp seeds.

Nutrition Info: Calories: 280 Cal ;Fat: 6 g :Carbs: 30 g ;Protein: 7 g ;Fiber: 2 g

Orange French Toast

Servings: 4

Cooking Time: 10 Minutes

Ingredients:

- ➢ 3 very ripe bananas
- ➢ 1 cup unsweetened nondairy milk
- ➢ zest and juice of 1 orange
- ➢ 1 teaspoon ground cinnamon
- ➢ ¼ teaspoon grated nutmeg
- ➢ 4 slices french bread, 1 tablespoon coconut oil

Directions:

- ➢ In a blender, combine the bananas, almond milk, orange juice and zest, cinnamon, and nutmeg, then blend until smooth. Pour the mixture into a 9-by-13-inch baking dish. Soak the bread in the mixture for 5 minutes on each side.
- ➢ While the bread soaks, heat a griddle or sauté pan over medium-high heat. Melt the coconut oil in the pan and swirl to coat. Cook the bread slices until golden brown on both sides for about 5 minutes each. Serve immediately.

Nutrition Info: Calories: 116 Cal ;Fat: 1 g :Carbs: 20 g ;Protein: 5 g ;Fiber: 1 g

Tropical French Toasts

Servings: 4

Cooking Time: 55 Minutes

Ingredients:

- 2 tbsp flax seed powder
- 1 ½ cups unsweetened almond milk
- ½ cup almond flour
- 2 tbsp maple syrup + extra for drizzling
- 2 pinches of salt
- ½ tbsp cinnamon powder
- ½ tsp fresh lemon zest
- 1 tbsp fresh pineapple juice
- 8 whole-grain bread slices

Directions:

- Preheat the oven to 400 F and lightly grease a roasting rack with olive oil. Set aside.
- In a medium bowl, mix the flax seed powder with 6 tbsp water and allow thickening for 5 to 10 minutes. Whisk in the almond milk, almond flour, maple syrup, salt, cinnamon powder, lemon zest, and pineapple juice. Soak the bread on both sides in the almond milk mixture and allow sitting on a plate for to 3 minutes.

> ➢ Heat a large skillet over medium heat and place the bread in the pan. Cook until golden brown on the bottom side. Flip the bread and cook further for until golden brown on the other side, 4 minutes in total. Transfer to a plate, drizzle some maple syrup on top and serve immediately.

Nutrition Info: Calories: 116 Cal ;Fat: 1 g :Carbs: 20 g ;Protein: 5 g ;Fiber: 1 g

Quinoa Applesauce Muffins

Servings: 5

Cooking Time: 15 Minutes

Ingredients:

➢ 2 tablespoons coconut oil or margarine, melted, plus more for coating the muffin tin

➢ ¼ cup ground flaxseed

➢ ½ cup water

➢ 2 cups unsweetened applesauce

➢ ½ cup brown sugar

➢ 1 teaspoon apple cider vinegar

➢ 2½ cups whole-grain flour

➢ 1½ cups cooked quinoa

➢ 2 teaspoons baking soda

➢ Pinch salt

➢ ½ cup dried cranberries or raisins

Directions:

➢ Preparing the Ingredients.

➢ Preheat the oven to 400°F.

➢ Coat a muffin tin with coconut oil, line with paper muffin cups, or use a nonstick tin. In a large bowl, stir together the flaxseed and water. Add the applesauce, sugar, coconut oil, and vinegar. Stir to combine. Add the flour, quinoa, baking soda, and salt, stirring until just combined. Gently fold in the cranberries without stirring too much. Scoop the muffin mixture into the prepared tin, about ⅓ cup for each muffin.

➢ Bake for 15 to 20 minutes, until slightly browned on top and springy to the touch. Let cool for about 10 minutes. Run a dinner knife around the inside of each cup to loosen, then tilt the muffins on their sides in the muffin wells so air gets underneath. These keep in an airtight container in the refrigerator for up to 1 week or in the freezer indefinitely.

Nutrition Info: Per Serving:(1muffin): Calories: 387; Protein: 7g; Total fat: 5g; Saturated fat: 2g; Carbohydrates: 57g; Fiber: 8g

Grits With Fried Tofu And Avocado

Servings: 3

Cooking Time: 30 Minutes

Ingredients:

➢ 3 teaspoons sesame oil

➢ 12 ounces firm tofu, cubed

➢ 1 small white onion, chopped

➢ 1/2 teaspoon turmeric

➢ 1/2 teaspoon red pepper flakes

➢ 3 cups water

➢ 1 cup stone-ground corn grits

➢ 1 thyme sprig

➢ 1 rosemary sprig

➢ 1 bay leaf

➢ 1/4 cup nutritional yeast

➢ 1 medium tomato, sliced

➢ 1 medium avocado, pitted, peeled and sliced

Directions:

➢ Heat the sesame oil in a wok over a moderately high heat. Now, fry your tofu for about 6 minutes.

➢ Add in the onion, turmeric and red pepper and continue cooking until the tofu is crisp on all sides and the onion is tender and translucent.

➢ In a saucepan, place the water, grits, thyme sprig, rosemary sprig and bay leaf and bring to a boil. Tun the heat to a simmer, cover and let it cook for approximately 20 minutes or until the most of the water is absorbed.

➢ Add in the nutritional yeast and stir to combine well.

➢ Divide the grits between serving bowls and top with the fried tofu/onion mixture. Top with tomato and avocado, salt to taste and serve immediately. Bon appétit!

Nutrition Info: Per Serving: Calories: 466; Fat: 27g; Carbs: 29.4g; Protein: 26.6g

Chocolate Granola Bars

Servings: 12

Cooking Time: 40 Minutes

Ingredients:

- ➢ 1 1/3 cups old-fashioned oats
- ➢ 1/2 cup fresh dates, pitted and mashed
- ➢ 1/2 cup dried cherries
- ➢ 1/3 cup agave syrup
- ➢ 1/3 cup almond butter, room temperature
- ➢ 2 tablespoons coconut oil, melted
- ➢ 1/2 cup almonds
- ➢ 1/2 cup walnuts
- ➢ 1/4 cup pecans
- ➢ 1/2 teaspoon allspice
- ➢ A pinch of salt
- ➢ A pinch of grated nutmeg
- ➢ 1/2 cup dark chocolate chunks

Directions:

- ➢ In a mixing bowl, thoroughly combine the oats, dates and dried cherries.
- ➢ Add in the agave syrup, almond butter and coconut oil. Stir in the nuts, spices and chocolate.

➢ Press the mixture into a lightly greased baking dish. Transfer it to your refrigerator for about minutes.

➢ Slice into 12 even bars and store in airtight containers. Enjoy!

Nutrition Info: Per Serving: Calories: 229; Fat: 13.4g; Carbs: 27.9g; Protein: 3.1g

Easy Homemade Chunky Applesauce

Servings: 5

Cooking Time: 20 Minutes

Ingredients:

- ➢ 7 medium McIntosh, Empire or different apples (around 3 pounds)
- ➢ 1/2 cup sugar
- ➢ 1/2 cup water
- ➢ 1 tablespoon lemon juice
- ➢ 1/4 teaspoon almond or vanilla concentrate
- ➢ Fueled by Chicory

Directions:

- ➢ Strip, center and cut every apple into 8 wedges. Cut each wedge across down the middle, place in a huge pan. Include remaining fixings.
- ➢ Heat to the point of boiling. Diminish excitement; stew, secured until wanted consistency is come to, 15- minutes, mixing once in a while.

Nutrition Info: Calories: 126 Cal ;Fat: 3g :Carbs: 10 g ;Protein: 2 g ;Fiber: 1 g

Power Green Smoothie

Servings: 2

Cooking Time: 10 Minutes

Ingredients:

- ➢ 1 banana, sliced
- ➢ 2 cups kale
- ➢ 1 cup sliced kiwi
- ➢ 1 orange, cut into segments
- ➢ 1 cup unsweetened coconut milk

Directions:

- ➢ Put in a food processor the banana, kale, kiwi, orange, and coconut milk. Pulse until smooth. Serve right away in glasses.

Nutrition Info: Calories: 126 Cal; Fat: 2g: Carbs: 15 g; Protein: 2 g ;Fiber: 1 g

Spicy Apple Pancakes

Servings: 4

Cooking Time: 30 Minutes

Ingredients:

- ➤ 2 cups almond milk
- ➤ 1 tsp apple cider vinegar
- ➤ 2 ½ cups whole-wheat flour
- ➤ 2 tbsp baking powder
- ➤ ½ tsp baking soda
- ➤ 1 tsp sea salt
- ➤ ½ tsp ground cinnamon
- ➤ ¼ tsp grated nutmeg
- ➤ ¼ tsp ground allspice
- ➤ ½ cup applesauce
- ➤ 1 cup water
- ➤ 1 tbsp coconut oil

Directions:

- ➤ Whisk the almond milk and apple cider vinegar in a bowl and set aside. In another bowl, combine the flour, baking powder, baking soda, salt, cinnamon, nutmeg, and allspice. Transfer the almond mixture to another bowl and beat with the applesauce and water.

➢ Pour in the dry ingredients and stir. Melt some coconut oil in a skillet over medium heat. Pour a ladle of the batter and cook for 5 minutes, flipping once until golden. Repeat the process until the batter is exhausted. Serve warm.

Nutrition Info: Calories: 236 Cal; Fat: 6g: Carbs: 18 g; Protein: 8 g ;Fiber: 1 g

Chocolate Chip And Coconut Pancakes

Servings: 4

Cooking Time: 20 Minutes

Ingredients:

- ➢ 2 bananas, sliced
- ➢ ¾ cup buckwheat flour
- ➢ 1 tablespoon coconut flakes, unsweetened
- ➢ 2 tablespoons rolled oats, old-fashioned
- ➢ 1/8 teaspoon sea salt
- ➢ 1/2 tablespoon baking powder
- ➢ 1/3 cup mini chocolate chips, grain-sweetened
- ➢ 1/4 cup maple syrup
- ➢ 1 teaspoon vanilla extract, unsweetened
- ➢ 1/2 tablespoon flaxseeds
- ➢ 1/4 cup of water
- ➢ 1/2 cup applesauce, unsweetened
- ➢ 1 cup almond milk, unsweetened

Directions:

- ➢ Take a small saucepan, place it over medium heat, add flaxseeds, pour in water, stir until mixed and cook for 3 minutes or until sticky mixture comes together.

- ➢ Then immediately strain the flaxseed mixture into a cup, discard the seeds, and set aside until required.
- ➢ Take a large bowl, add oats and flour in it, stir in salt, baking powder, and coconut flakes and then whisk until combined.
- ➢ Take another bowl, add flax seed reserve along with maple syrup, vanilla, applesauce, and milk and then whisk until combined.
- ➢ Transfer this mixture into the oat-flour mixture, stir until combined, and then fold in chocolate chips until mixed.
- ➢ Take a skillet pan, place it over medium-low heat, spray it with oil and when hot, pour in one-fourth of the batter, spread gently into a pancake shape, and cook for 5 minutes per side until golden brown on both sides.
- ➢ Transfer pancake to a plate and repeat with the remaining batter.
- ➢ Serve pancakes with sliced banana.

Nutrition Info: Calories: 284 Cal; Fat: 7g: Carbs: 22 g; Protein: 10 g ;Fiber: 4 g

Cherry And Poppy Seed Muffins

Servings: 2

Cooking Time: 30 Minutes

Ingredients:

- 1 cup (120 g) raw buckwheat flour
- 1 ¼ cup oatmeal (155 g) oatmeal
- 2 tablespoons poppy seeds
- 2 teaspoons cinnamon
- ½ teaspoon cardamom
- 2 teaspoons baking powder
- Wet
- 10 chopped figs
- A little more than 1 cup (260 ml) of vegetable milk, without sugar
- 2 ripe bananas
- 2 heaped tablespoons unsweetened applesauce
- 2 tablespoons peanut butter
- 1 pinch of sea salt (optional)
- ½ cup (50 g) dark chocolate (at least 70% cocoa), chopped
- 24 fresh or frozen cherries

Directions:

- Preheat the oven to 0 ° C (355 ° F).

- ➤ Cut the figs and soak them in vegetable milk for at least 30 minutes. If you want to dip it further, put it in the refrigerator.
- ➤ While the figs are soaked, chop the chocolate and place it aside. Put all other dry ingredients in a bowl. Put the figs and milk into the mixer. Add all remaining wet ingredients and mix until smooth.
- ➤ Pour the wet mixture over the dry ingredients and mix well. Make sure there are no lumps. Add chopped chocolate.
- ➤ The mold is filled with 12 muffins (molded using silicon) with a lump and finally hits two cherries in each muffin.
- ➤ Bake for 25-30 minutes. Allow it to cool a little before trying to remove it from the mold.

Nutrition Info: Calories: 304 Cal; Fat: 7g: Carbs: 19 g; Protein: 8 g ;Fiber: 3 g

Mixed Berry And Almond Butter Swirl Bowl

Servings: 3

Cooking Time: 10 Minutes

Ingredients:

- ➢ 1 ½ cups almond milk
- ➢ 2 small bananas
- ➢ 2 cups mixed berries, fresh or frozen
- ➢ 3 dates, pitted, 3 scoops hemp protein powder
- ➢ 3 tablespoons smooth almond butter
- ➢ 2 tablespoons pepitas

Directions:

- ➢ In your blender or food processor, mix the almond milk with the bananas, berries and dates.
- ➢ Process until everything is well combined. Divide the smoothie between three bowls.
- ➢ Top each smoothie bowl with almond butter and use a butter knife to swirl the almond butter into the top of each smoothie bowl.
- ➢ Afterwards, garnish each smoothie bowl with pepitas, serve well-chilled and enjoy!

Nutrition Info: Per Serving: Calories: 397; Fat: 16.3g; Carbs: 48.5g; Protein: 19.6g

Savory Oatmeal Porridge

Servings: 4

Cooking Time: 25 Minutes

Ingredients:

- ➢ 2½ cups vegetable broth
- ➢ 2½ cups unsweetened almond milk or other plant-based milk
- ➢ ½ cup steel-cut oats
- ➢ 1 tablespoon farro
- ➢ ½ cup slivered almonds
- ➢ ¼ cup nutritional yeast
- ➢ 2 cups old-fashioned rolled oats
- ➢ ½ teaspoon salt (optional)

Directions:

- ➢ Preparing the Ingredients
- ➢ In a large saucepan or pot, bring the broth and almond milk to a boil. Add the oats, farro, almond slivers, and nutritional yeast. Cook over medium-high heat for minutes while stirring occasionally.
- ➢ Add the rolled oats and cook for another 5 minutes until creamy. Stir in the salt (if using).
- ➢ Finish and Serve
- ➢ Divide into 4 single-serving containers.

➢ Let cool before sealing the lids. Place the airtight containers in the refrigerator for 5 days or freeze for up to 3 months. To thaw, refrigerate overnight. Reheat in the microwave for 2½ minutes or in a skillet over medium-high heat for to 8 minutes.

Nutrition Info: Per Serving: Calories: 208; Protein: 14g; Total fat: 8g; Saturated fat: 1g; Carbohydrates: 22g; Fiber: 7g

Mango And Pineapple Smoothie

Servings: 1

Cooking Time: 0 Minute

Ingredients:

- 3/4 cup mango chunks, frozen
- 1 cup sliced cucumber
- 1 cup pineapple chunks, frozen
- 2 cups fresh spinach
- 1 scoop of vanilla protein powder
- 1 teaspoon moringa powder
- 1 teaspoon pure vanilla extract, unsweetened
- 1 2/3 cup almond milk, unsweetened

Directions:

- Place all the ingredients in the order in a food processor or blender and then pulse for 2 to 3 minutes at high speed until smooth.
- Pour the smoothie into a glass and then serve.

Nutrition Info: Calories: 335 Cal ;Fat: 11 g :Carbs: 50 g ;Protein: 4 g ;Fiber: 2 g

Great Green Smoothie

Servings: 4

Cooking Time: 0 Minutes

Ingredients:

- ➢ 4 bananas, peeled
- ➢ 4 cups hulled strawberries
- ➢ 4 cups spinach
- ➢ 4 cups plant-based milk

Directions:

- ➢ Preparing the Ingredients.
- ➢ Open 4 quart-size, freezer-safe bags. In each, layer in the following order: 1 banana (halved or sliced), 1 cup of strawberries, and 1 cup of spinach. Seal and place in the freezer.
- ➢ To serve, take a frozen bag of Great Green Smoothie ingredients and transfer to a blender. Add 1 cup of plant-based milk, and blend until smooth. Place freezer bags in the freezer for up to 2 months.

Nutrition Info: Calories: 104 Cal; Fat: 2g: Carbs: 8 g; Protein: 1 g ;Fiber: 4 g

Vanilla Crepes With Berry Cream Compote Topping

Servings: 4

Cooking Time: 35 Minutes

Ingredients:

- 1 knob plant butter
- 2 tbsp pure date sugar
- 1 tsp vanilla extract
- ½ cup fresh blueberries
- ½ cup fresh raspberries
- ½ cup whipped coconut cream
- 2 tbsp flax seed powder
- 1 tsp vanilla extract
- 1 tsp pure date sugar
- ¼ tsp salt
- 2 cups almond flour
- 1 ½ cups almond milk
- 1 ½ cups water
- 3 tbsp plant butter for frying

Directions:

- Melt butter in a pot over low heat and mix in the date sugar, and vanilla. Cook until the sugar melts and then, toss in berries. Allow softening for 2-3 minutes. Set aside to cool.

➤ In a medium bowl, mix the flax seed powder with 6 tbsp water and allow thickening for 5 minutes to make the flax egg. Whisk in vanilla, date sugar, and salt. Pour in a quarter cup of almond flour and whisk, then a quarter cup of almond milk, and mix until no lumps remain. Repeat the mixing process with the remaining almond flour and almond milk in the same quantities until exhausted.

➤ Mix in 1 cup of water until the mixture is runny like that of pancakes and add the remaining water until the mixture is lighter. Brush a large non-stick skillet with some butter and place over medium heat to melt. Pour 1 tablespoon of the batter in the pan and swirl the skillet quickly and all around to coat the pan with the batter. Cook until the batter is dry and golden brown beneath, about seconds.

➤ Use a spatula to carefully flip the crepe and cook the other side until golden brown too. Fold the crepe onto a plate and set aside. Repeat making more crepes with the remaining batter until exhausted. Plate the crepes, top with the whipped coconut cream and the berry compote. Serve immediately.

Nutrition Info: Calories: 304 Cal; Fat: 7g: Carbs: 19 g; Protein: 8 g ;Fiber: 3 g

Mango Madness

Servings: 4

Cooking Time: 0 Minutes

Ingredients:

- ➢ 1 banana
- ➢ 1 cup chopped mango (frozen or fresh)
- ➢ 1 cup chopped peach (frozen or fresh)
- ➢ 1 cup strawberries
- ➢ 1 carrot, peeled and chopped (optional)
- ➢ 1 cup water

Directions:

- ➢ Preparing the Ingredients.
- ➢ Purée everything in a blender until smooth, adding more water if needed.
- ➢ If you can't find frozen peaches, and fresh ones aren't in season, just use extra mango or strawberries, or try cantaloupe.

Nutrition Info: Per Serving: Calories: 376; Protein: 5g; Total fat: 2g; Carbohydrates: 95g; Fiber: 14g

Mexican-style Omelet

Servings: 2

Cooking Time: 15 Minutes

Ingredients:

- ➢ 2 tablespoons olive oil
- ➢ 1 small onion, chopped
- ➢ 2 Spanish peppers, deseeded and chopped
- ➢ 1/2 cup chickpea flour
- ➢ 1/2 cup water
- ➢ 3 tablespoons rice milk, unsweetened
- ➢ 2 tablespoons nutritional yeast
- ➢ Kala namak salt and ground black pepper, to taste
- ➢ 1/2 teaspoon dried Mexican oregano
- ➢ 1/4 cup salsa

Directions:

- ➢ Heat the olive oil in a frying pan over medium-high flame. Once hot, sauté the onion and peppers for about 3 minutes until tender and aromatic.
- ➢ Meanwhile, whisk the chickpea flour with the water, milk, nutritional yeast, salt, black pepper and dried Mexican oregano.

➤ Then, pour the mixture into the frying pan.

➤ Cook for about minutes. Turn it over and cook for an additional 3 to 4 minutes until set. Serve with salsa and enjoy!

Nutrition Info: Per Serving: Calories: 329; Fat: 16.4g; Carbs: 35.2g; Protein: 12.9g

Omelet With Mushrooms And Peppers

Servings: 4

Cooking Time: 30 Minutes

Ingredients:

- ➢ 4 tablespoons olive oil
- ➢ 1 red onion, minced
- ➢ 1 red bell pepper, sliced
- ➢ 1 teaspoon garlic, finely chopped
- ➢ 1 pound button mushrooms, sliced
- ➢ Sea salt and ground black pepper, to taste
- ➢ 1/2 teaspoon dried oregano
- ➢ 1/2 teaspoon dried dill
- ➢ 16 ounces tofu, drained and crumbled
- ➢ 2 tablespoons nutritional yeast
- ➢ 1/2 teaspoon turmeric powder
- ➢ 4 tablespoons corn flour
- ➢ 1/3 cup oat milk, unsweetened

Directions:

- ➢ Preheat 2 tablespoons of the olive oil in a nonstick skillet over medium-high heat. Then, cook the onion and pepper for about 4 minutes until tender and fragrant.

51

- ➤ Add in the garlic and mushrooms and continue to sauté an additional to 3 minutes or until aromatic. Season with salt, black pepper, oregano and dill. Reserve.
- ➤ In your blender or food processor, mix the tofu, nutritional yeast, turmeric powder, corn flour and milk. Process until you have a smooth and uniform paste.
- ➤ In the same skillet, heat 1 tablespoon of the olive oil until sizzling. Pour in 1/2 of the tofu mixture and spread it with a spatula.
- ➤ Cook for about 6 minutes or until set; flip and cook it for another 3 minutes. Slide the omelet onto a serving plate.
- ➤ Spoon 1/2 of the mushroom filling over half of the omelet. Fold the unfilled half of omelet over the filling.
- ➤ Repeat with another omelet. Cut them into halves and serve warm. Bon appétit!

Nutrition Info: Per Serving: Calories: 390; Fat: 26.2g; Carbs: 22.4g; Protein: 22.1g

Baked Banana French Toast With Raspberry Syrup

Servings: 8

Cooking Time: 30 Minutes

Ingredients:

- ➤ FOR THE FRENCH TOAST
- ➤ 1 banana
- ➤ 1 cup coconut milk
- ➤ 1 teaspoon pure vanilla extract
- ➤ ¼ teaspoon ground nutmeg
- ➤ ½ teaspoon ground cinnamon
- ➤ 1½ teaspoons arrowroot powder
- ➤ Pinch sea salt
- ➤ 8 slices whole-grain bread
- ➤ FOR THE RASPBERRY SYRUP
- ➤ 1 cup fresh or frozen raspberries, or other berries
- ➤ 2 tablespoons water, or pure fruit juice
- ➤ 1 to 2 tablespoons maple syrup, or coconut sugar (optional)

Directions:

- ➤ Preparing the Ingredients
- ➤ Preheat the oven to 350°F.

➢ In a shallow bowl, purée or mash the banana well. Mix in the coconut milk, vanilla, nutmeg, cinnamon, arrowroot, and salt.

➢ Dip the slices of bread in the banana mixture, and then lay them out in a 13-by-9-inch baking dish. They should cover the bottom of the dish and can overlap a bit but they shouldn't be stacked on top of each other. Pour any leftover banana mixture over the bread and put the dish in the oven.

➢ Bake about 30 minutes, or until the tops are lightly browned. Serve topped with raspberry syrup. To Make the Raspberry Syrup

➢ Heat the raspberries in a small pot with the water and the maple syrup (if using) on medium heat.

➢ Leave to simmer, stirring occasionally and breaking up the berries, for 15 to 20 minutes until the liquid has reduced.

➢ Leftover raspberry syrup makes a great topping for simple oatmeal as a quick and delicious breakfast, or as a drizzle on top of some whole-grain toast smeared with natural peanut butter.

Nutrition Info: Per Serving: Calories: 166; Protein: 5g; Total fat: 7g; Saturated fat: 1g; Carbohydrates: 23g;

Chickpea Omelet With Spinach And Mushrooms

Servings: 4

Cooking Time: 15 Minutes

Ingredients:

- ➢ 1 cup chickpea flour
- ➢ ½ tsp onion powder
- ➢ ½ tsp garlic powder
- ➢ ¼ tsp white pepper
- ➢ ¼ tsp black pepper
- ➢ 1/3 cup nutritional yeast
- ➢ ½ tsp baking soda
- ➢ 1 small green bell pepper, deseeded and chopped
- ➢ 3 scallions, chopped
- ➢ 1 cup sautéed sliced white button mushrooms
- ➢ ½ cup chopped fresh spinach
- ➢ 1 cup halved cherry tomatoes for serving
- ➢ 1 tbsp fresh parsley leaves

Directions:

- ➢ In a medium bowl, mix the chickpea flour, onion powder, garlic powder, white pepper, black pepper, nutritional yeast, and baking soda until well combined.

➢ Heat a medium skillet over medium heat and add a quarter of the batter. Swirl the pan to spread the batter across the pan. Scatter a quarter each of the bell pepper, scallions, mushrooms, and spinach on top, and cook until the bottom part of the omelet sets and is golden brown, 1 to minutes. Carefully, flip the omelet and cook the other side until set and golden brown.

➢ Transfer the omelet to a plate and make the remaining omelets using the remaining batter in the same proportions.

➢ Serve the omelet with the tomatoes and garnish with the parsley leaves. Serve.

Nutrition Info: Calories: 204 Cal; Fat: 6g: Carbs: 13 g; Protein: 10 g ;Fiber: 3 g

Spicy Quinoa Bowl With Black Beans

Servings: 4

Cooking Time: 25 Minutes

Ingredients:

- ➢ 1 cup brown quinoa, rinsed
- ➢ 3 tbsp plant-based yogurt
- ➢ ½ lime, juiced
- ➢ 2 tbsp chopped fresh cilantro
- ➢ 1 (5 oz) can black beans, drained
- ➢ 3 tbsp tomato salsa, ¼ avocado, sliced
- ➢ 2 radishes, shredded
- ➢ 1 tbsp pepitas (pumpkin seeds)

Directions:

- ➢ Cook the quinoa with 2 cups of slightly salted water in a medium pot over medium heat or until the liquid absorbs, minutes. Spoon the quinoa into serving bowls and fluff with a fork.
- ➢ In a small bowl, mix the yogurt, lime juice, cilantro, and salt. Divide this mixture on the quinoa and top with the beans, salsa, avocado, radishes, and pepitas. Serve immediately

Nutrition Info: Calories: 204 Cal; Fat: 6g: Carbs: 22 g; Protein: 12 g; Fiber: 3 g

Wild Ginger Green Smoothie

Servings: 1

Cooking Time: 0 Minute

Ingredients:

- ➢ 1/2 cup pineapple chunks, frozen
- ➢ 1/2 cup chopped kale
- ➢ 1/2 frozen banana
- ➢ 1 tablespoon lime juice
- ➢ 2 inches ginger, peeled, chopped
- ➢ 1/2 cup coconut milk, unsweetened
- ➢ 1/2 cup coconut water

Directions:

- ➢ Place all the ingredients in the order in a food processor or blender and then pulse for 2 to 3 minutes at high speed until smooth.
- ➢ Pour the smoothie into a glass and then serve.

Nutrition Info: Calories: 331 Cal ;Fat: 14 g :Carbs: 40 g ;Protein: 16 g ;Fiber: 9 g

Banana Bread Rice Pudding

Servings: 4

Cooking Time: 50 Minutes

Ingredients:

➤ 1cup brown rice

➤ 1½ cups water

➤ 1½ cups nondairy milk

➤ 3 tablespoons sugar (omit if using a sweetened nondairy milk)

➤ 2 teaspoons pumpkin pie spice or ground cinnamon

➤ 2 bananas

➤ 3 tablespoons chopped walnuts or sunflower seeds (optional)

Directions:

➤ Preparing the Ingredients

➤ In a medium pot, combine the rice, water, milk, sugar, and pumpkin pie spice. Bring to a boil over high heat, turn the heat to low, and cover the pot. Simmer, stirring occasionally, until the rice is soft and the liquid is absorbed. White rice takes about minutes; while brown rice takes about 50 minutes to cook.

➢ Smash the bananas and stir them into the cooked rice.

➢ Finish and Serve

➢ Serve topped with walnuts (if using). Leftovers will keep refrigerated in an airtight container for up to days.

Nutrition Info: Per Serving: Calories: 479; Protein: 9g; Total fat: 13g; Saturated fat: 1g; Carbohydrates: 86g; Fiber: 7g

Root Vegetable Hash With Avocado Crème

Servings: 3

Cooking Time: 10 Minutes

Ingredients:

- 1/2 c onion, diced
- 1 T vegan butter
- 2 cloves garlic, minced
- 1 c sweet potatoes, diced
- 1 c turnips, diced
- 1 c broccoli florets, diced
- 2 vegan sausages, diced
- 1 c collard greens, chopped
- 1/2 tsp sea salt
- 1 tsp cumin
- 1/2 tsp black pepper
- 1/4 – 1/2c vegetable stock
- 1/4 c fresh cilantro, chopped
- 1 medium avocado
- 1 T balsamic vinegar
- 1/4 c cashews

Directions:

➤ Melt and hest the butter in a skillet. Add onion and garlic and sauté until they are translucent about 5 minutes.

➤ Add sweet potatoes and turnips stir to match. Cook for 5-8 minutes.

➤ Add the broccoli and vegetables. Continue cooking until it turns light green and start to soften for 5 to 8 minutes.

➤ Add the roasted field, salt, pepper, cumin, coriander, and vinegar. Reduce the heat and get it cooked until the meat is hot and the flavors melt.

➤ Mix the avocado, cashews, and vegetable broth in a blender until smooth.

➤ Plate and serve with a spoonful of avocado cream on top. Garnish with more cilantro.

Nutrition Info: 19 g fat 30 g of carbohydrates 17 g protein 7 g sugar 691 mg sodium

General Tso's Cauliflower

Servings: 4

Cooking Time: 20 Minutes

Ingredients:

- ➢ Oil for profound fat fricasseeing
- ➢ 1/2 cup generally useful flour
- ➢ 1/2 cup cornstarch
- ➢ 1 teaspoon salt
- ➢ 1 teaspoon preparing powder
- ➢ 3/4 cup club pop
- ➢ 1 medium head cauliflower, cut into 1-inch florets (around 6 cups)
- ➢ Sauce:
- ➢ 1/4 cup squeezed orange
- ➢ 3 tablespoons sugar
- ➢ 3 tablespoons soy sauce
- ➢ 3 tablespoons vegetable stock
- ➢ 2 tablespoons rice vinegar
- ➢ 2 teaspoons sesame oil
- ➢ 2 teaspoons cornstarch
- ➢ 2 tablespoons canola oil
- ➢ 2 to 6 dried pasilla or other hot chilies, cleaved

➢ 3 green onions, white part minced, green part daintily cut

➢ 3 garlic cloves, minced

➢ 1 teaspoon ground new gingerroot

➢ 1/2 teaspoon ground orange get-up-and-go

➢ 4 cups hot cooked rice

Directions:

➢ In an electric skillet or profound fryer, heat oil to 375°. Consolidate flour, cornstarch, salt, and heating powder. Mix in club soft drink just until mixed (hitter will be slender). Plunge florets, a couple at once, into the player and fry until cauliflower is delicate and covering is light dark colored, 8- minutes. Channel on paper towels.

➢ For the sauce, whisk together the initial six fixings; race in cornstarch until smooth.

➢ In a huge pot, heat canola oil over medium-high warmth. Include chilies; cook and mix until fragrant, 2 minutes. Include a white piece of onions, garlic, ginger, and orange get-up-and-go; cook until fragrant, around 1 moment. Mix soy sauce blend; add to the pan. Heat to the point of boiling; cook and mix until thickened, 4 minutes.

➢ Add cauliflower to sauce; hurl to cover. Present with rice; sprinkle with daintily cut green onions.

Nutrition Info: Calories: 204 Cal; Fat: 6g: Carbs: 22 g; Protein: 12 g; Fiber: 3 g

Chia Smoothie

Servings: 3

Cooking Time: 0 Minutes

Ingredients:

- ➢ 1 banana
- ➢ ½ cup coconut milk, 1 cup water
- ➢ 1 cup alfalfa sprouts (optional)
- ➢ 1 to 2 soft Medjool dates, pitted
- ➢ 1 tablespoon chia seeds, or ground flax or hemp hearts
- ➢ ¼ teaspoon ground cinnamon, Pinch ground cardamom, 1 tablespoon grated fresh ginger, or ¼ teaspoon ground ginger

Directions:

- ➢ Purée everything in a blender until smooth, adding more water (or coconut milk) if needed.
- ➢ Although dates are super sweet, they don't cause a large blood sugar spike. They're great to boost sweetness while also boosting your intake of fiber and potassium.

Nutrition Info: Per Serving: Calories: 477; Protein: 7g; Total fat: 29g; Carbohydrates: 57g; Fiber: 14g

Fruit Salad With Lemon-ginger Syrup

Servings: 4

Cooking Time: 10 Minutes

Ingredients:

- ➢ 1/2 cup fresh lemon juice
- ➢ 1/4 cup agave syrup
- ➢ 1 teaspoon fresh ginger, grated
- ➢ 1/2 teaspoon vanilla extract
- ➢ 1 banana, sliced
- ➢ 2 cups mixed berries, 1 cup seedless grapes
- ➢ 2 cups apples, cored and diced

Directions:

- ➢ Bring the lemon juice, agave syrup and ginger to a boil over medium-high heat. Then, turn the heat to medium-low and let it simmer for about 6 minutes until it has slightly thickened.
- ➢ Remove from the heat and stir in the vanilla extract. Allow it to cool.
- ➢ Layer the fruits in serving bowls. Pour the cooled sauce over the fruit and serve well chilled. Bon appétit!

Nutrition Info: Per Serving: Calories: 164; Fat: 0.5g; Carbs: 42g; Protein: 1.4g

Hot Pink Smoothie

Servings: 1

Cooking Time: 0 Minute

Ingredients:

- ➢ 1 clementine, peeled, segmented
- ➢ 1/2 frozen banana
- ➢ 1 small beet, peeled, chopped
- ➢ 1/8 teaspoon sea salt
- ➢ 1/2 cup raspberries
- ➢ 1 tablespoon chia seeds
- ➢ 1/4 teaspoon vanilla extract, unsweetened
- ➢ 2 tablespoons almond butter
- ➢ 1 cup almond milk, unsweetened

Directions:

- ➢ Place all the ingredients in the order in a food processor or blender and then pulse for 2 to 3 minutes at high speed until smooth.
- ➢ Pour the smoothie into a glass and then serve.

Nutrition Info: Calories: 278 Cal; Fat: 5.6 g :Carbs: 37.2 g ;Protein: 6.2 g ;Fiber: 13.2 g

Scrambled Tofu With Bell Pepper

Servings: 4

Cooking Time: 20 Minutes

Ingredients:

- ➢ 2 tbsp plant butter, for frying
- ➢ 1 (14 oz) pack firm tofu, crumbled
- ➢ 1 red bell pepper, chopped
- ➢ 1 green bell pepper, chopped
- ➢ 1 tomato, finely chopped
- ➢ 2 tbsp chopped fresh green onions
- ➢ Salt and black pepper to taste
- ➢ 1 tsp turmeric powder
- ➢ 1 tsp Creole seasoning
- ➢ ½ cup chopped baby kale
- ➢ ¼ cup grated plant-based Parmesan

Directions:

- ➢ Melt the plant butter in a large skillet over medium heat and add the tofu. Cook with occasional stirring until the tofu is light golden brown while making sure not to break the tofu into tiny bits but to have scrambled egg resemblance, 5 minutes.

➤ Stir in the bell peppers, tomato, green onions, salt, black pepper, turmeric powder, and Creole seasoning. Sauté until the vegetables soften, 5 minutes. Mix in the kale to wilt, 3 minutes and then, half of the plant-based Parmesan cheese. Allow melting for 1 to minutes and then turn the heat off. Top with the remaining cheese and serve warm.

Nutrition Info: Calories: 228 Cal; Fat: 5.6 g :Carbs: 21 g ;Protein: 10.2 g ;Fiber: 7.2 g

Warm Quinoa Breakfast Bowl

Servings: 4

Cooking Time: 0 Minutes

Ingredients:

- ➢ 3 cups freshly cooked quinoa
- ➢ 1⅓ cups unsweetened soy or almond milk
- ➢ 2 bananas, sliced
- ➢ 1 cup raspberries
- ➢ 1 cup blueberries
- ➢ ½ cup chopped raw walnuts

Directions:

- ➢ Preparing the Ingredients
- ➢ Divide the ingredients among 4 bowls, starting with a base of ¾ cup quinoa, ⅓ cup milk, ½ banana, ¼ cup raspberries, ¼ cup blueberries, and tablespoons walnuts.

Nutrition Info: Calories: 218 Cal; Fat: 4.6 g :Carbs: 21 g ;Protein: 10.2 g ;Fiber: 5.2 g

Tropical Smoothie In A Bowl

Servings: 2

Cooking Time: 0 Minutes

Ingredients:

- ➢ 2 cups frozen mango pieces
- ➢ ½ cup frozen pineapple chunks
- ➢ 1 frozen banana, ½ to 1 cup of vegetable milk
- ➢ 2 tablespoons chopped nuts of your choice
- ➢ ¼ cup chopped fruit of your choice
- ➢ Additional aderts
- ➢ 1 tablespoon flaxseed flour
- ➢ 1½ tablespoons coconut pieces

Directions:

- ➢ Add the mango, pineapple, banana and vegetable milk (cup creates a thinner shake, and ½ cup makes it thicker) in a blender and mix everything until you get a smooth mixture.
- ➢ Put the smoothie into a bowl and cover it with nuts and fruit.

Nutrition Info: Calories: 125 Cal; Fat: 2.6 g :Carbs: 11 g ;Protein: 4.2 g ;Fiber: 3.2 g

Grandma's Breakfast Waffles

Servings: 4

Cooking Time: 20 Minutes

Ingredients:

- 1 cup all-purpose flour
- 1/2 cup spelt flour
- 1 teaspoon baking powder
- A pinch of salt
- 1/4 teaspoon ground cinnamon
- 1/4 teaspoon grated nutmeg
- 1/2 teaspoon vanilla extract
- 1 cup almond milk, unsweetened
- 2 tablespoons blackstrap molasses
- 2 tablespoons coconut oil, melted
- 1 tablespoon fresh lime juice

Directions:

- Preheat a waffle iron according to the manufacturer's instructions.
- In a mixing bowl, thoroughly combine the flour, baking powder, salt, cinnamon, nutmeg and vanilla extract.

- ➤ In another bowl, mix the liquid ingredients. Then, gradually add in the wet mixture to the dry mixture.
- ➤ Beat until everything is well blended.
- ➤ Ladle 1/4 of the batter into the preheated waffle iron and cook until the waffles are golden and crisp. Repeat with the remaining batter.
- ➤ Serve your waffles with a fruit compote or coconut cream, if desired. Bon appétit!

Nutrition Info: Per Serving: Calories: 316; Fat: 9.9g; Carbs: 50.4g; Protein: 8.3g

Homemade Toast Crunch

Servings: 8

Cooking Time: 15 Minutes

Ingredients:

- ➤ 1 cup almond flour
- ➤ 1 cup coconut flour
- ➤ 1/2 cup all-purpose flour
- ➤ 1 cup sugar
- ➤ 1 teaspoon kosher salt
- ➤ 1 teaspoon cardamom
- ➤ 1/4 teaspoon grated nutmeg
- ➤ 1 tablespoon cinnamon
- ➤ 3 tablespoons flax seeds, ground
- ➤ 1/2 cup coconut oil, melted
- ➤ 8 tablespoons coconut milk

Directions:

- ➤ Begin by preheating the oven to 340 degrees F. In a mixing bowl, thoroughly combine all the dry ingredients.
- ➤ Gradually pour in the oil and milk; mix to combine well.
- ➤ Shape the dough into a ball and roll out between 2 sheets of a parchment paper. Cut into small

squares and prick them with a fork to prevent air bubbles.

➢ Bake in the preheated oven for about 15 minutes. They will continue to crisp as they cool. Bon appétit!

Nutrition Info: Per Serving: Calories: 330; Fat: 25.7g; Carbs: 24.7g; Protein: 4.8g

Strawberry Limeade

Servings: 6

Cooking Time: 5 Minutes

Ingredients:

- ➢ 2 cup strawberries
- ➢ 1 cup sugar or as per taste
- ➢ 7 cups of water
- ➢ 2 cup lemon juice
- ➢ Sliced berries for garnish

Directions:

- ➢ Take a small bowl, add sugar and water and put in microwave until dissolved. Now take a blender and add strawberries and a cup of water and blend well. Combine the strawberries puree with the sugar dissolve water and mix. Pour lime juice and water if required. Stir well and chill before serving. You can add berries on the top as garnishing.

Nutrition Info: Calories: 144, carbohydrates: 37g, sugar: 35g

Pink Panther Smoothie

Servings: 3

Cooking Time: 0 Minutes

Ingredients:

- ➢ 1 cup strawberries
- ➢ 1 cup chopped melon (any kind)
- ➢ 1 cup cranberries, or raspberries
- ➢ 1 tablespoon chia seeds
- ➢ ½ cup coconut milk, or other non-dairy milk
- ➢ 1 cup water
- ➢ 1 teaspoon goji berries (optional)
- ➢ 2 tablespoons fresh mint, chopped

Directions:

- ➢ Preparing the Ingredients.
- ➢ Purée everything in a blender until smooth, adding more water (or coconut milk) if needed.
- ➢ Add bonus boosters, as desired. Purée until blended. If you don't have coconut, try using sunflower seeds for an immune boost of zinc and selenium.

Nutrition Info: Per Serving: 3 Cups Calories: 459; Protein: 8g; Total fat: 30g; Carbohydrates: 52g; Fiber: 19g

Cranberry Oat Cookies

Servings: 2

Cooking Time: 20 Minutes

Ingredients:

➢ ½ cup rolled oats

➢ 1 tbsp whole-wheat flour

➢ ½ tsp baking powder

➢ 2 tbsp pure date sugar

➢ ½ tsp ground cinnamon

➢ ¼ cup applesauce

➢ 2 tbsp dried cranberries

Directions:

➢ Combine the oats, flour, baking powder, sugar, and cinnamon in a bowl. Add in applesauce and cranberries. Stir until well combined. Form 2 cookies out of the mixture and microwave for ½ minutes. Allow to cool before serving.

Nutrition Info: Calories: 275 Cal; Fat: 6.6 g :Carbs: 18 g ;Protein: 5.2 g ;Fiber: 6.2 g

Healthy Breakfast Bowl

Servings: 2

Cooking Time: 10 Minutes

Ingredients:

- ➢ 1 vegan yogurt
- ➢ 1/2 avocado (peeled and diced)
- ➢ 1 handful blueberries
- ➢ 1 tablespoon cacao nibs
- ➢ 1 handful of strawberries
- ➢ 1 tablespoon mulberries
- ➢ 1 tablespoon goji berries
- ➢ 1 tablespoon desiccated coconut

Directions:

- ➢ Put the avocado in a nice bowl.
- ➢ Top up with vegan yogurt.
- ➢ Sprinkle the remaining ingredients and enjoy it.

Nutrition Info: carbohydrates: 55 g calories: 471 Fat: 25g sodium: 183 g protein: 11 g sugar: 32 g

Pumpkin Steel-cut Oats

Servings: 4

Cooking Time: 35 Minutes

Ingredients:

- ➤ 3 cups water
- ➤ 1 cup steel-cut oats
- ➤ ½ cup canned pumpkin purée
- ➤ ¼ cup pumpkin seeds (pepitas)
- ➤ 2 tablespoons maple syrup
- ➤ Pinch salt

Directions:

- ➤ Preparing the Ingredients.
- ➤ In a large saucepan, bring the water to boil.
- ➤ Add the oats, stir, and reduce the heat to low. Simmer until the oats are soft, for 20 to minutes, continuing to stir occasionally.
- ➤ Stir in the pumpkin purée and continue cooking on low for 3 to 5 minutes. Stir in the pumpkin seeds and maple syrup, and season with salt.
- ➤ Finish and Serve
- ➤ Divide the oatmeal into 4 single-serving containers. Let it cool before sealing the lids.

➢ Place the airtight containers in the refrigerator for 5 days or freeze for up to 3 months. To thaw, refrigerate overnight. Reheat in the microwave for 2½ minutes or in a skillet over medium-high heat for 6 to 8 minutes.

Nutrition Info: Per Serving: Calories:121; Protein: 4g; Total fat: 5g; Carbohydrates: 17g; Fiber: 2g

Plant Based Cookbook: Breakfast Recipes

Scrambled Eggs With Aquafaba

Servings: 2

Cooking Time: 15 Minutes

Ingredients:

- ➢ 6 ounces tofu, firm, pressed, drained
- ➢ 1/2 cup aquafaba
- ➢ 1 1/2 tablespoons olive oil
- ➢ 1 tablespoon nutritional yeast
- ➢ 1/4 teaspoon black salt
- ➢ 1/8 teaspoon ground turmeric
- ➢ 1/4 teaspoon ground black pepper

Directions:

- ➢ Take a food processor, add tofu, yeast, black pepper, salt, and turmeric, then pour in aquafaba and olive oil and pulse for minute until smooth.
- ➢ Take a skillet pan, place it over medium heat, and when hot, add tofu mixture and cook for 1 minute.
- ➢ Cover the pan, continue cooking for minutes, then uncover the pan and pull the mixture across the pan with a wooden spoon until soft forms.
- ➢ Continue cooking for 10 minutes until resembles soft scrambled eggs, folding tofu mixture gently

and heat over medium heat, then remove the pan from heat and season with salt and black pepper to taste.

➢ Serve straight away

Nutrition Info: Calories: 208 Cal ;Fat: 5.1 g :Carbs: 31.3 g ;Protein: 8.3 g ;Fiber: 10.4 g

Chocolate Pb Smoothie

Servings: 4

Cooking Time: 0 Minutes

Ingredients:

- 1 banana
- ¼ cup rolled oats
- 1 tablespoon flaxseed, or chia seeds
- 1 tablespoon unsweetened cocoa powder
- 1 tablespoon peanut butter, or almond or sunflower seed butter
- 1 tablespoon maple syrup (optional)
- 1 cup alfalfa sprouts, or spinach, chopped (optional) ,½ cup non-dairy milk (optional)
- 1 cup water, 1 teaspoon maca powder (optional)
- 1 teaspoon cocoa nibs(optional)

Directions:

- Purée everything in a blender until smooth, adding more water (or non-dairy milk) if needed. Add bonus boosters, as desired. Purée until blended.

Nutrition Info: Per Serving: Calories: 474; Protein: 13g; Total fat: 16g; Carbohydrates: 79g; Fiber: 18g

Strawberry, Banana And Coconut Shake

Servings: 1

Cooking Time: 0 Minute

Ingredients:

- ➢ 1 tablespoon coconut flakes
- ➢ 1 1/2 cups frozen banana slices
- ➢ 8 strawberries, sliced
- ➢ 1/2 cup coconut milk, unsweetened
- ➢ 1/4 cup strawberries for topping

Directions:

- ➢ Place all the ingredients in the order in a food processor or blender, except for topping and then pulse for 2 to 3 minutes at high speed until smooth.
- ➢ Pour the smoothie into a glass and then serve.

Nutrition Info: Calories: 335 Cal ;Fat: 5 g :Carbs: 75 g ;Protein: 4 g ;Fiber: 9 g

Peanut Butter And Jelly Smoothie

Servings: 2

Cooking Time: 5 Minutes

Ingredients:

- ➤ 1 cup frozen raspberries
- ➤ 1 cup frozen strawberries
- ➤ 1 serving collagen peptides
- ➤ 1 tbsp. peanut butter
- ➤ ¾ cup almond milk

Directions:

- ➤ Take a blender. Add in raspberries, strawberries, peanut butter, collagen peptide and almond milk. Blend all ingredients until well combined. Add almond milk as per the required consistency. Pour into smoothie serving glasses and top up with the peanut butter or anything of your choice for dressing.

Nutrition Info: Calories: 251, fat: 11.1g, carbohydrates: 27.5g, proteins: 15.7g

Polenta With Pears And Cranberries

Servings: 4

Cooking Time: 12 Minutes

Ingredients:

- ➢ 1 cup dried cranberries
- ➢ 1 teaspoon ground cinnamon
- ➢ 2 pears, peeled, cored, diced
- ➢ 1/4 cup brown rice syrup
- ➢ 2 cups of Polenta, warm

Directions:

- ➢ Take a medium saucepan, place it over medium heat, add rice syrup, and cook for 2 minutes until hot.
- ➢ Then add berries and pears, sprinkle with cinnamon, stir until mixed and cook for 10 minutes until tender.
- ➢ Distribute polenta among bowls, top with cooked berries mixture, and then serve.

Nutrition Info: Calories: 274, fat: 5.1g, carbohydrates: 21.5g, proteins: 6 g

Easy Omelet With Tomato And Hummus

Servings: 2

Cooking Time: 20 Minutes

Ingredients:

- 10 ounces silken tofu, pressed
- 4 tablespoons water
- 1 teaspoon balsamic vinegar
- 3 tablespoons nutritional yeast
- 2 teaspoons arrowroot powder
- 1/2 teaspoon turmeric powder
- Kala namak salt and black pepper
- 2 tablespoons olive oil
  - Topping:
- 2 tablespoons hummus
- 1 medium tomato, sliced
- 1 teaspoon garlic, minced
- 2 scallions, chopped

Directions:

- In your blender or food processor, mix the tofu, water, balsamic vinegar, nutritional yeast, arrowroot powder, turmeric powder, salt and black pepper. Process until you have a smooth and uniform paste.

➢ In a nonstick skillet, heat the olive oil until sizzling. Pour in 1/of the tofu mixture and spread it with a spatula.

➢ Cook for about 6 minutes or until set; flip and cook it for another minutes. Slide the omelet onto a serving plate.

➢ Repeat with the remaining batter. Place the topping ingredients over half of each omelet. Fold unfilled half of your omelet over the filling. Bon appétit!

Nutrition Info: Per Serving: Calories: 324; Fat: 20.3g; Carbs: 18.4g; Protein: 18g

Gingerbread Belgian Waffles

Servings: 3

Cooking Time: 25 Minutes

Ingredients:

> ➤ 1 cup all-purpose flour

> ➤ 1 teaspoon baking powder

> ➤ 1 tablespoon brown sugar

> ➤ 1 teaspoon ground ginger

> ➤ 1 cup almond milk

> ➤ 1 teaspoon vanilla extract

> ➤ 2 olive oil

Directions:

> ➤ Preheat a waffle iron according to the manufacturer's instructions.

> ➤ In a mixing bowl, thoroughly combine the flour, baking powder, brown sugar, ground ginger, almond milk, vanilla extract and olive oil.

> ➤ Beat until everything is well blended.

> ➤ Ladle 1/3 of the batter into the preheated waffle iron and cook until the waffles are golden and crisp. Repeat with the remaining batter.

> ➤ Serve your waffles with blackberry jam, if desired. Bon appétit!

Nutrition Info: Per Serving: Calories: 299; Fat: 12.6g; Carbs: 38.5g; Protein: 6.8g

Pumpkin Cake With Pistachios

Servings: 4

Cooking Time: 70 Minutes

Ingredients:

- ➢ 2 tbsp flaxseed powder
- ➢ 3 tbsp vegetable oil
- ➢ ¾ cup canned pumpkin puree
- ➢ ½ cup pure corn syrup
- ➢ 3 tbsp pure date sugar
- ➢ 1 ½ cups whole-wheat flour
- ➢ ½ tsp cinnamon powder
- ➢ ½ tsp baking powder
- ➢ ¼ tsp cloves powder
- ➢ ½ tsp allspice powder
- ➢ ½ tsp nutmeg powder
- ➢ 2 tbsp chopped pistachios

Directions:

- ➢ Preheat the oven to 350 F and lightly coat an 8 x 4-inch loaf pan with cooking spray. In a medium bowl, mix the flax seed powder with 6 tbsp water and allow thickening for 5 minutes to make the flax egg.

➢ In a bowl, whisk the vegetable oil, pumpkin puree, corn syrup, date sugar, and flax egg. In another bowl, mix the flour, cinnamon powder, baking powder, cloves powder, allspice powder, and nutmeg powder. Add this mixture to the wet batter and mix until well combined. Pour the batter into the loaf pan, sprinkle the pistachios on top, and gently press the nuts onto the batter to stick.

➢ Bake in the oven for 50-55 minutes or until a toothpick inserted into the cake comes out clean. Remove the cake onto a wire rack, allow cooling, slice, and serve.

Nutrition Info: Calories: 374, fat: 12.1g, carbohydrates: 21.5g, proteins: 6 g

Ciabatta Bread Pudding With Sultanas

Servings: 4

Cooking Time: 2 Hours 10 Minutes

Ingredients:

- 2 cups coconut milk, unsweetened
- 1/2 cup agave syrup
- 1 tablespoon coconut oil
- 1/2 teaspoon vanilla essence
- 1/2 teaspoon ground cardamom
- 1/4 teaspoon ground cloves
- 1/2 teaspoon ground cinnamon
- 1/4 teaspoon Himalayan salt
- 3/4 pound stale ciabatta bread, cubed
- 1/2 cup sultana raisins

Directions:

- In a mixing bowl, combine the coconut milk, agave syrup, coconut oil, vanilla, cardamom, ground cloves, cinnamon and Himalayan salt.
- Add the bread cubes to the custard mixture and stir to combine well. Fold in the sultana raisins and allow it to rest for about 1 hour on a counter.
- Then, spoon the mixture into a lightly oiled casserole dish.

➤ Bake in the preheated oven at 350 degrees F for about 1 hour or until the top is golden brown.

➤ Place the bread pudding on a wire rack for 10 minutes before slicing and serving. Bon appétit!

Nutrition Info: Per Serving: Calories: 458; Fat: 10.4g; Carbs: 81.3g; Protein: 11.4g

Chocolate Oat Smoothie

Servings: 1

Cooking Time: 0 Minute

Ingredients:

- ¼ cup rolled oats
- 1 ½ tablespoon cocoa powder, unsweetened
- 1 teaspoon flax seeds
- 1 large frozen banana
- 1/8 teaspoon sea salt
- 1/8 teaspoon cinnamon
- ¼ teaspoon vanilla extract, unsweetened
- 2 tablespoons almond butter
- 1 cup coconut milk, unsweetened

Directions:

- Place all the ingredients in the order in a food processor or blender and then pulse for 2 to 3 minutes at high speed until smooth.
- Pour the smoothie into a glass and then serve.

Nutrition Info: Calories: 262 Cal ;Fat: 7.3 g :Carbs: 50.4 g ;Protein: 8.1 g ;Fiber: 9.6 g

Creole Tofu Scramble

Servings: 4

Cooking Time: 10 Minutes

Ingredients:

- ➢ 2 tbsp plant butter, for frying
- ➢ 1 (14 oz) pack firm tofu, pressed and crumbled
- ➢ 1 medium red bell pepper, deseeded and chopped
- ➢ 1 medium green bell pepper, deseeded and chopped
- ➢ 1 tomato, finely chopped
- ➢ 2 tbsp chopped fresh green onions
- ➢ Salt and black pepper to taste
- ➢ 1 tsp turmeric powder
- ➢ 1 tsp Creole seasoning
- ➢ ½ cup chopped baby kale
- ➢ ¼ cup grated plant-based Parmesan cheese

Directions:

- ➢ Melt the plant butter in a large skillet over medium heat and add the tofu. Cook with occasional stirring until the tofu is light golden brown while making sure not to break the tofu into tiny bits but to have scrambled egg resemblance, 5 minutes.

- Stir in the bell peppers, tomato, green onions, salt, black pepper, turmeric powder, and Creole seasoning. Sauté until the vegetables soften, 5 minutes.
- Mix in the kale to wilt, minutes and then, half of the plant-based Parmesan cheese. Allow melting for 1 to 2 minutes and then turn the heat off.
- Dish the food, top with the remaining cheese, and serve warm.

   Nutrition Info: Calories: 274, fat: 5.1g, carbohydrates: 21.5g, proteins: 6 g

Coconut & Raspberry Pancakes

Servings: 4

Cooking Time: 25 Minutes

Ingredients:

- 2 tbsp flax seed powder
- ½ cup coconut milk
- ¼ cup fresh raspberries, mashed
- ½ cup oat flour
- 1 tsp baking soda
- A pinch salt
- 1 tbsp coconut sugar
- 2 tbsp pure date syrup
- ½ tsp cinnamon powder
- 2 tbsp unsweetened coconut flakes
- 2 tsp plant butter
- Fresh raspberries for garnishing

Directions:

- In medium bowl, mix the flax seed powder with the 6 tbsp water and allow thickening for 5 minutes. Mix in coconut milk and raspberries. Add the oat flour, baking soda, salt, coconut sugar, date syrup, and cinnamon powder. Fold in the coconut flakes until well combined.

➢ Working in batches, melt a quarter of the butter in a non-stick skillet and add ¼ cup of the batter. Cook until set beneath and golden brown, minutes. Flip the pancake and cook on the other side until set and golden brown, 2 minutes. Transfer to a plate and make the remaining pancakes using the rest of the ingredients in the same proportions. Garnish the pancakes with some raspberries and serve warm!

Nutrition Info: Calories: 374, fat: 5.1g, carbohydrates: 19.5g, proteins: 10 g

Lightning Source UK Ltd.
Milton Keynes UK
UKHW020625210621
385893UK00013B/1318